D0736169

BABE RUTH

GREAT AMERICANS IN SPORTS

BABE RUTH

MATT CHRISTOPHER

Little, Brown and Company

New York Boston

Little, Brown and Company

Hachette Book Group
1290 Avenue of the Americas, New York, NY 10104
Visit us at lb-kids.com

mattchristopher.com

Little, Brown and Company is a division of Hachette Book Group, Inc. The Little, Brown name and logo are trademarks of Hachette Book Group, Inc.

The publisher is not responsible for websites (or their content) that are not owned by the publisher.

First Great Americans in Sports Edition: September 2015
Originally published as *Babe Ruth: Legends in Sports* in September 2005 by Little, Brown and Company

Text revised and updated by Zachary Rau
Cover illustration by Michael Cho

Matt Christopher® is a registered trademark of Matt Christopher Royalties, Inc.

Library of Congress Cataloging-in-Publication Data

Christopher, Matt, 1917–1997.
Great Americans in sports, Babe Ruth / Matt Christopher.
pages cm
ISBN 978-0-316-26097-8 (paperback) — ISBN 978-0-316-26098-5 (ebook) — ISBN 978-0-316-26099-2 (library edition ebook) 1. Ruth, Babe, 1895–1948— Juvenile literature. 2. Baseball players—United States—Biography— Juvenile literature. I. Title.
GV865.R8C55 2015
796.357092—dc23
[B]
2015007627

10 9 8 7 6 5 4 3 2 1

RRD-C

Printed in the United States of America

CONTENTS

INTRODUCTION

December 26, 1919, is a day that will live in infamy in baseball lore. No pennants were lifted, no championships won. In fact, there wasn't even a game being played. Yet on that day, the history of baseball was forever changed. It was the day the greatest player to ever play the game was traded from the Boston Red Sox to the New York Yankees, their fiercest rivals. After helping Boston to three World Series wins as the league's best left-handed pitcher, including back-to-back wins in 1915 and 1916, George Herman "Babe" Ruth was sold to the hated Yankees for $125,000.

Babe Ruth's talent was unmistakable. He could play in outfield, he could hit with power and for average, and he could pitch. In Boston he was a twenty-four-game winner in 1917, but could he fit in to a new locker room? The Yankees thought so. They thought he could be the best player in the league, and they were right. But they didn't expect him to become one of the best baseball players of all time.

The season after being sold to the Yankees, the Babe had a breakout year as a hitter. That year, he drove in 137 RBIs, collected 172 hits, and added 150 base on balls, all while striking out only 80 times. His .376 average was fourth best in the league that season, and his 158 runs and 54 home runs were top in both categories. His 54 homers were twice as many as the second-place finisher in that category. That was just the beginning of a career that helped establish the Yankees as the most decorated and famous franchise in major league baseball history.

The Bambino would go on to lead the Yankees to seven pennants and four World Series titles over his fourteen-year career. He hit more home runs and drove in more RBIs than anyone else playing the game in the 1920s and 1930s. It would take almost forty years after the Babe retired for Hank Aaron to break the Babe's all-time home run record. Before Babe, the league was dominated by crafty pitchers like Christy Mathewson of the New York Giants, or flamethrowers like Walter Johnson of the Washington Senators, but after the year Babe was sold, for what was at the time a huge amount of money, he changed the sport into a game where the long ball was king and every game drew larger crowds than the last. Babe Ruth was the first true sports superstar.

When the Boston Red Sox owner Harry Frazee sold the Babe, he unknowingly helped create the Yankees as we know them today: a storied franchise that has set the standard for all other teams. But he had also sealed the Red Sox's fate. Along with selling the Babe, Frazee also traded Wally Schang, Waite Hoyt, Harry Harper, and Mike McNally to the Yankees. It was almost as though Frazee wanted the Yankees to be better than the Red Sox. That off-season, Red Sox fans everywhere began to despise the Yankees for "stealing" all their best players. After having won five of the last fifteen World Series titles, the Boston Red Sox went on to experience a series of near misses, late-game blunders, mishaps, and heartbreaking late-season collapses. It would take the Red Sox more than eighty years to win the World Series again. Everyone called it the Curse of the Bambino. The fans blamed Harry Frazee for upsetting the gods of baseball. And those gods cursed the Boston Red Sox for selling the best player to ever play the game. That was the beginning of one of the most ferocious rivalries in all of sports. The Babe changed everything.

A teammate of Babe Ruth's once said, "I saw a man transformed from a human being into something pretty close to a god."

Indeed, Babe Ruth is one of baseball's legendary figures, a player unlike anyone before or since. His home runs changed the game forever. His personality was bigger than the game. His behavior off the field almost forced him out of the game before he ever had the chance to be great. There will never, ever be another ballplayer like the Babe.

CHAPTER ONE
1895–1914

FROM THE STREET TO ST. MARY'S

No amount of awards, statistics, or championships could ever truly tell the tale of the great Babe Ruth. He was as famous for his exploits off the field as he was for his play on it. The fans loved him for his hitting, but he was also a generous man, always ready with a smile for the men, women, and children who came to cheer him on. He knew how to play to the crowd. He was a born showman. Babe never lost sight of the fact that baseball was a game meant to be *played*. Barrel-chested with a wide mouth and a broad nose that dominated his face, Babe Ruth lived his life and played the game like an oversized kid, with simple and pure love for the sport. And his joy was infectious to anyone who saw him play. Even today, more than half a century after his death in 1948, he remains the most popular baseball player of all time.

Maybe his carefree and showy attitude was a

product of his upbringing, a hard and tough one on the streets of Baltimore, Maryland.

Born on February 6, 1895, George Herman Ruth Jr. was the first of eight children born to German Americans George and Kate Ruth. From the start, the young family had a rough time. George Ruth Sr. struggled to find work while Kate stayed home alone with their son. But George Jr.'s mother was in poor health. Her illnesses prevented her from giving George the attention and structure that an active and adventurous child needed. And when his sister Mary Margaret was born, five-year-old George was left to take care of himself as best he could.

Later in his life, Babe Ruth would admit that he "was a bad kid." He would say that he "had no sense of right or wrong." Every morning he took to the streets with other unlucky boys. Although they often played children's games, including baseball, without adult supervision, they frequently caused trouble. They stole food and money, committed vandalism, chewed tobacco, and fought among themselves or against children from other neighborhoods.

Young George rarely went to school. His parents tried to force him to go, but even beatings with a leather strap couldn't make him obey. Every day he became more uncontrollable. When he wasn't on the streets, he hung around the saloon his father owned—hardly a good place for a young boy to grow up. At an age when he should have been learning to read and write, he was drinking alcohol, smoking, and stealing whiskey from customers.

One night, when George was seven years old, police officers were called to break up a brawl in his father's saloon. Afterward, a neighbor told the authorities she had noticed that George was in the saloon when he should have been attending school. The Ruths were ordered to send George to St. Mary's Industrial School for Boys not far from the Chesapeake Bay.

Operated by the Xaverian Brothers of the Catholic Church, St. Mary's was a training school for orphans, delinquents, and other boys in need of help. More than eight hundred boys, ranging in age from seven to eighteen, lived and studied at St. Mary's. Discipline under the brothers was strict. The boys were told what to do and when to do it. The students referred to themselves as "inmates," and they all slept in big dormitories and were not allowed to leave the campus without proper supervision.

Young George arrived at St. Mary's on June 13,

1902. The imposing gray stone buildings and high wooden fence made the school look like a prison. When he first arrived, George didn't understand what St. Mary's was or why he was there. His father escorted him to the school office, said good-bye, and left him behind. The foul-mouthed, tobacco-chewing street urchin suddenly discovered he wasn't so tough. Alone and afraid, George began to cry.

Fortunately, the Xaverian Brothers understood young boys like George. George wasn't bad as much as he was wild. He just needed someone to pay attention to him and provide him with some direction, discipline, and love. The monks tried to offer each boy an opportunity at an education and a trade. Skilled tradesmen had an easier time finding work, which the monks believed would help the boys become responsible and upstanding citizens.

Teaching a strong work ethic was part of the St. Mary's philosophy. George was kept so busy at the school that he didn't have time to get into trouble. Every St. Mary's boy was expected to wake up by six each day to attend morning church services. After church was breakfast and then the boys spent five hours in school, either learning academic subjects or studying for a trade. After a two-hour break for lunch and exercise, they spent another two hours either in class or working a job. Before dinner the boys were encouraged to play sports. They were then allowed to read for forty-five minutes before going to bed at eight fifteen. Every boy attended school five days a week plus a half day on Saturdays. After church services on Sundays the boys were free to participate in school sports, play in the band, and take part in other similar activities.

At first, George hated St. Mary's. No one had ever told him when to get up in the morning, when to eat, what to wear or do, or when to go to bed. After all, he had always done as he pleased before, and now suddenly the brothers were telling him what to do every minute of the day. It was a struggle for George to settle into the routine at first, but with a bit of help he managed to fit right in.

To oversee each boy's progression through St. Mary's, every Xaverian Brother was assigned eight to ten boys to watch over and mentor. Brother Matthias was the head of discipline at St. Mary's and was assigned to look after young George Ruth. Brother Matthias was an enormous man. He stood nearly six and a half feet tall and weighed about three hundred pounds. Matthias looked as if he could break a person in half with his bare hands. But Brother Matthias didn't need to use force. He was firm, but gentle and patient. Although the boys called him "the boss," they did so out of fondness rather than fear because he treated each student with respect.

Brother Matthias took a special interest in young George, who could neither read nor write when he started attending St. Mary's. Ever so slowly, George began to respond to the attention. No adult had ever taken an interest in him, and he began working hard at school and in his shirt-making classes. A word or look of praise from Brother Matthias was all it took to make George swell with pride.

Brother Matthias loved baseball and was a good player himself at one time. He wowed the students at St. Mary's by hitting long fly balls while holding the bat with only one hand. It was at St. Mary's that young George learned to play America's favorite pastime. Just like Brother Matthias, George found that he also loved the game. Nearly every afternoon, he played pickup games or practiced batting. On the weekends, he played for several teams run by St. Mary's. These teams were made up of players of different ages from the various shop programs and dormitories. Some of the teams represented St. Mary's in games against other institutions. From Saturday afternoon through Sunday, George often played games with five or six different teams.

In no time at all, it was clear that George was one of the best players at St. Mary's. He was big for his age, coordinated, wiry, and strong. Although he played all positions, his strong arm often earned him a place behind the plate as a catcher. A natural lefty, George didn't mind wearing the catcher's mitt on the wrong hand. Instead, he perfected a method of catching the ball, flipping the glove in the air, tucking it under his right arm, then snagging the ball with his throwing hand. Even with the extra time it took to complete this juggling maneuver, his arm was so powerful he could still throw out runners trying to steal. And he could hit the stuffing out of the ball.

Some of Brother Matthias's most important life lessons were actually taught on the baseball diamond. One day the pitcher on George's team was getting hit hard, and George started laughing at him and making mean comments. Brother Matthias saw what was happening and said, "All right, George. *You* pitch."

George's eyes widened and his jaw dropped. "I— I don't know how to pitch," he stammered.

"You must know a lot about pitching," Brother Matthias replied, "to know that your friend isn't any good. Go out there and show us how it is done."

George realized Matthias was serious. He walked to the mound and took the ball from the pitcher. He stood on the mound, awkwardly shuffling his feet as the other boys laughed at him.

But they didn't laugh for long. George may not have known a lot about pitching, but he had a cannon for an arm. He picked up pitching quickly and from then on took regular turns on the mound. He had also learned an important lesson. Being on a team meant supporting your teammates and the team whether you were winning or losing—especially when you were losing.

George did so well at St. Mary's that he was periodically sent home to live with his family on a trial basis. But without the structure and discipline of St. Mary's, he soon fell back into bad habits. Before long his father would send him back to St. Mary's, where Brother Matthias was always waiting to welcome him back.

When George was thirteen, he was sent home to live with his family again. This time, he managed to stay out of serious trouble for almost two years.

Then his mother died. Seeing how hard George had taken his mother's death, his father returned him to St. Mary's for good. George was scheduled to stay at St. Mary's until he was twenty-one years old and an adult in the eyes of the law.

Apart from a few scrapes with other boys, George rarely got into trouble at St. Mary's. While he wasn't much of a student, he had beautiful handwriting and was one of the best shirtmakers at the school. Years later, he would brag to his major league teammates that he could make a shirt in fifteen minutes. They'd all smirk when they saw him carefully ironing his shirts. Sometimes George's teammates would even bring him their own laundry to iron!

The other boys at St. Mary's were always thrilled when he came back. With George Ruth on their team, St. Mary's was difficult to beat. Not only was he the best pitcher at the school, he was also the best hitter. In one season he hit more than sixty home runs!

Soon he was too good for the competition provided by St. Mary's opponents. Brother Matthias arranged for George to play ball on the weekends for local amateur and semipro teams made up of other teenagers and young men. Stories about the young ballplayer named Ruth began to appear in

Baltimore newspapers. By 1913, he was one of the best-known amateur players in the Baltimore area.

The best team in Baltimore was the professional Baltimore Orioles of the International League. Owner Jack Dunn, known as a shrewd judge of talent, scoured the surrounding areas for potential ballplayers.

During the summer of 1913, former major league pitcher Joe Engel saw eighteen-year-old George pitch a game against Mount St. Mary's, a local college team. George struck out eighteen of the first twenty men he faced. Engel immediately knew that George, who now stood six feet two inches tall and weighed 170 pounds, was something special.

The next day, Engel bumped into Dunn. He told him about the left-handed pitcher named Ruth and said, "He's got real stuff."

Engel had Dunn's ear. His opinion was well respected inside the Orioles. Several other youngsters from St. Mary's had done well in professional baseball. So in February of 1914, Dunn paid a visit to St. Mary's.

The Orioles were about to start spring training, and Dunn needed to stock his team with prospects. He met with Brother Paul, St. Mary's superintendent, and told him he was interested in signing the young left-handed pitcher with the "stuff." Brother Paul wasn't surprised. For several months there had been rumors that Dunn was interested in George. With Brother Paul's permission, George worked out for Dunn privately. The club owner was impressed and wanted to sign him.

There was just one problem. George was only nineteen years old. St. Mary's was George's legal guardian and he was supposed to stay at the school until age twenty-one. But Brother Paul was a baseball fan, too, and he knew that a chance to play professional baseball was a wonderful opportunity for George. He made arrangements to make Jack Dunn George's legal guardian.

Dunn offered George a contract of six hundred dollars for the season. That isn't much money now, but for George that was striking it rich. George couldn't believe it. He had never imagined that it was possible to be *paid* to play baseball. George had never had more than a dollar or two in his pocket. Six hundred dollars seemed like a king's ransom. He couldn't wait to sign the contract.

George gathered up the few belongings he owned in a cheap suitcase, walked with Dunn out of St. Mary's, and headed for spring training in Fayetteville,

North Carolina. He paused outside the large iron gate and said good-bye to Brother Matthias, thanking him for all his help. George was excited, but Brother Matthias could tell he was a little scared, too. It reminded Matthias of when George had first arrived at St. Mary's years earlier. Matthias told him not to worry. "You'll make it, George," he said. Then George walked off with Dunn.

On February 27, 1914, the last entry under the name George Ruth in St. Mary's records reads simply, *He is going to join Balt. Baseball team.*

Mark Rucker/Transcendental Graphics / Getty Images

THE ST. MARY'S TEAM POSES FOR A PORTRAIT SOMETIME DURING 1910–1912. BABE IS IN THE TOP ROW, FAR LEFT.

CHAPTER TWO
1914

DUNN'S BABE

When George left St. Mary's, he knew very little of the world outside of Baltimore. He had never been away from the city before. He had never lived alone, bought his own clothes, or cooked his own meals. All he knew how to do was play baseball and make shirts—and follow the daily routine at St. Mary's.

On the train ride south to North Carolina, George spent most of his time gazing out the window, trying to take it all in. In a matter of days, his entire life had changed. When it was time to go to bed, one of the Oriole players had to explain to him how to fold down the sleeping berth. He also played a trick on the young rookie.

In the berth was a small mesh clothes hammock. The veteran player told George, "That's for your pitching arm." When George went to bed, he dutifully placed his left arm in the hammock. When he woke up the next morning, his arm was stiff and sore from hanging in a hammock all night. The veterans all got a good laugh when they saw him rubbing his arm.

After the team checked into their hotel in Fayetteville, they went to the dining room for breakfast. George looked at the menu and wasn't quite sure what to do next. He didn't have much money in his pocket and had never ordered from a menu. A veteran saw the puzzled look on his face and explained that the team paid for their meals during spring training. "Order anything you want," he told him.

George couldn't believe it. He ordered pancakes and ham, wolfed them down, and then ordered another helping. He made quick work of the second order, and then asked for a third stack of pancakes and more ham. His teammates had long since finished eating and just stared at him in wonder. He ate pancake after pancake after pancake. His teammates had never seen anyone eat so much.

Everything was brand-new to George. He had never seen an elevator and was fascinated by it. He could be found riding it up and down for hours. He had never ridden a bicycle, either, and every time he saw one he jumped on for a teetering ride.

The other players couldn't help but laugh at him. They had never seen anyone have so much fun. He was like a gigantic kid.

Once he was out on the ball field, however, the laughter stopped. George was impressive both on the mound and at the plate. In one scrimmage on March 7, George walloped a home run into the cornfield beyond right field. Local fans recalled only one other ball hit like that, by former Olympian and major leaguer Jim Thorpe when he had played minor league baseball in Fayetteville. George's blast traveled some sixty feet farther than Thorpe's had. A headline in one Baltimore newspaper announced: RUTH MAKES MIGHTY CLOUT. In a few more seasons, such headlines would become familiar.

All spring, George was the big story for the Orioles. After only two weeks in spring training Dunn told a newspaper, "Babe Ruth will definitely be staying with the team."

The story of how George got the nickname is uncertain, but according to most accounts, his Baltimore teammates dubbed him "Babe" because he was so young and inexperienced, like a baby. They called him "Dunn's babe." George wasn't bothered by the nickname, and though the newspapers would still call him George for years to come, everyone who knew him called him Babe.

Dunn always thought of Babe Ruth as his ace pitcher. Just three weeks after Babe joined the Orioles, Dunn tapped him to pitch an exhibition game against the Philadelphia Athletics, the defending world champions. Most rookie pitchers would have been nervous, but not Babe. He barely followed major league baseball at St. Mary's and didn't even know the names of the players. Although the Athletics peppered him with thirteen hits, Babe stayed cool and held them to only two runs. The Orioles won the game by a score of 6–2 and beat the champs!

The regular season began in late April. The Orioles returned to Baltimore and Babe received his first paycheck. With fifty dollars in his pocket, Babe immediately went out and bought a motorcycle. Although Dunn was scared his rookie phenom would crash and get hurt, he couldn't keep Babe off the bike. The sight of Babe Ruth tearing around the city on the bike soon became familiar to those who lived in Baltimore.

Babe pitched his first regular season game on

April 22 against the Buffalo Bisons. After a shaky start, he settled down and threw a six-hit shutout, and also hit two singles. The Orioles won that game 6–0.

Unfortunately, hardly anyone saw Babe play. One year earlier, a new major league, the Federal League, had placed a team in Baltimore called the Terrapins. The new team stole Baltimore's attention, and local baseball fans all but ignored the Orioles. Dunn knew that unless the Orioles started drawing some fans, he would soon go broke.

Dunn hoped the fact that Babe was a Baltimore native would lure fans to the park to see a home-town star. Although Babe didn't win every game he pitched, he was clearly one of the best rookies in the league. By mid-May, Dunn became concerned that the Terrapins would try to lure Babe away with a big salary, so he tripled the star rookie's pay to $1,800 for the season.

The Orioles were able to put together an impressive winning streak in June, winning thirteen games in a row on the backs of Babe Ruth and fellow rookie pitcher Ernie Shore. Yet Baltimore fans continued to ignore the Orioles—and Dunn was losing money fast. Even though the Federal League was also having financial trouble, Dunn was afraid he would run out of cash before the season was over. In early July, despite the fact that Baltimore was in first place, Dunn decided to sell players' contracts to raise some money. Within a few days, Babe Ruth, Ernie Shore, and catcher Ben Egan's contracts were purchased by the Boston Red Sox for a total of $25,000.

The Red Sox were one of the most successful franchises in baseball, winning world championships in both 1903 and 1912. In 1914, the Red Sox had decided to rebuild for the future and began adding talented young players to the roster. Owner Joseph Lannin and manager Bill Carrigan hoped that Ruth and Shore would anchor the pitching staff for years to come.

Babe left for Boston by train, arriving at Back Bay Station on the morning of July 11. Over the course of six months, he had gone from being a student at St. Mary's Industrial School for Boys to a professional baseball player for one of the strongest teams in the major leagues. But despite this huge change, Babe Ruth himself stayed much the same—a big kid.

As soon as he arrived in Boston, he checked into

a hotel and then looked for a place to eat. He found Landers Coffee Shop and ordered a big meal. As he ate, he told his waitress, a young woman named Helen Woodford, all about his trip to Boston.

Babe Ruth would return to Landers many times in the next months and become very close to Helen. But this first time he couldn't stay long to chat. Fenway Park was calling his name.

CHAPTER THREE
1914–1918

BOSTON'S BABE

The Red Sox were in sixth place with a record of 40–38 when Babe Ruth joined the team. The season looked lost. Manager Bill Carrigan was already looking ahead to next season and wanted to see how close his new players were to being able to help the team win. When the Babe arrived at Fenway Park on July 11, 1914, Carrigan told him to get warm because he was going to start against the Cleveland Indians.

Some players might have been nervous to start their first game for a popular team like the Red Sox, but not Babe. His calmness came partly from his laid-back personality and partly from the fact that there wasn't a lot of pressure on him: the Sox were in sixth place and no one expected a win. Over the first six innings, though, Babe held the Indians in check, giving up only six hits and one run before running out of gas in the seventh inning. Babe got his first W in a red uniform that day as the Sox beat the Indians 4–3.

However, over the next month Carrigan rarely used Babe Ruth. Before he became a regular on the mound, he needed to break some bad habits. For example, Babe's tongue would curl into the corner of his mouth when he was going to throw a curveball. This was something Babe hadn't noticed he was doing, but professional hitters picked it up right away and tried to exploit it.

Carrigan was just as concerned with Babe's adjustments to big-league life. Away from home, in a big city alone for the first time and making lots of money, Babe began to fall back into his bad habits. He stayed out all night, often letting his new "friends" take advantage of him and his newfound money.

His teammates didn't quite know what to think of the newcomer. He was obviously a talented ballplayer, but he didn't behave like a rookie. Most young players are intimidated by older players. But Babe insisted on taking batting practice, something pitchers, particularly rookie pitchers, just didn't do. When the veterans complained, Babe stood up to them. He argued with umpires, and on one occasion was even thrown out of a game. He didn't bother to learn anyone's name and called everyone "kid," even players much older than himself. In the clubhouse he played practical jokes and tried to get other players to wrestle.

Off the field, Babe was still learning how to act and behave. On the road, he shared a hotel room with Ernie Shore. When he confronted Babe about using his toothbrush, Babe quipped, "That's all right. I don't mind." Shore just shook his head in wonder. Babe could be frustrating, but it was hard to stay angry with him for long. Everyone could see that he was just a big kid trying to grow up in a hurry.

In mid-August, the Red Sox arranged to send Babe to another club owned by Joseph Lannin in Providence, Rhode Island. The Providence Grays of the International League were fighting for a pennant and they needed pitching for the stretch. Babe needed to pitch, too, since he couldn't get any better by continuing to sit on the bench. He had to play, and the Red Sox knew it.

Babe was sad to leave Boston, but Providence was only forty miles to the south. Babe's arm gave the Grays a much-needed boost. He learned fast, and over the remainder of the season won nine out of ten games. Given the time to play, Babe found his rhythm as a pitcher.

On September 5, during a game he was pitching masterfully, Babe Ruth stepped up to the plate and crushed a ball over the outfield wall. It was his first professional home run and showed that this rookie could hit. That would change everything. With a little luck and a lot of help from Babe, the Grays went on to win the International League pennant.

After the Grays' final victory, Babe Ruth rejoined Boston for the last ten days of the Red Sox season. He also went to visit Helen, the waitress he had met when he first arrived. One day, while eating his usual enormous breakfast at Landers, Babe turned to Helen while still chewing a huge mouthful of food and said, "Hey, hon, how about you and me getting married?" It wasn't the most romantic proposal in history, but to Helen it was all she needed. She said yes, and they married in Baltimore soon after the season ended.

In March of 1915, Babe and his teammates arrived for spring training in Hot Springs, Arkansas. He worked to secure a place as one of the team's best pitchers, while his batting performances during practice and exhibition games began to attract attention. In that era of the game, the home run was a rarity. Players who hit ten or twelve home runs over an entire season were considered power hitters. The prevailing baseball philosophy during the years that Babe broke into the game was based on the principles of "small ball" baseball. Most batters just tried to make contact and get base hits. The next batter would try to get a hit or advance the runner—a hit and run.

But not the Babe. He swung for the fences on every pitch and didn't seem worried when he missed the ball. In fact, fans enjoyed watching him swing and miss almost as much as they enjoyed watching him connect. When he missed a pitch, he spun almost completely around, which looked funny from the stands. When he did hit the ball, it was a spectacle to behold. The ball shot off the bat and soared through the sky longer and farther than anyone had ever seen.

Babe had quickly developed a reputation as one of the most talented young players in the game, but also as one of the most problematic. Off the field, he was a terror. Hot Springs was a party town and Babe stayed out all hours of the night. Bill Carrigan tried to keep him in check with small fines and lectures, but the Babe usually paid him little attention. He was now twenty-one years old, an official adult. He enjoyed doing whatever he wanted, and he wanted to do it all. His appetites for food, drink, and tobacco were all larger than life, just like the Babe.

Ruth opened his second season as one of Boston's top pitchers, but in his first four games he managed only one win. It was on May 6 that he turned his season—and perhaps his career—around. Carrigan picked him to start against the New York Yankees. At the time, the Yankees didn't have their own field. They played at the cavernous Polo Grounds, the home ballpark of the New York Giants. The Polo Grounds was a pitcher's park, where the fences were relatively close right down the lines, but the deepest in the league everywhere else. At the Polo Grounds, it was far more common to hit an inside-the-park home run rather than hitting one over the fence. After two scoreless innings, Babe came to bat in the third against pitcher Jack Warhop.

It didn't matter where he played, the Babe kept swinging for the fences. Warhop delivered a pitch, and Babe swung as hard as he could. The ball hit the bat squarely and a loud *crack* echoed through the park. The drive soared high to right center field and just kept going, up and up, before finally landing in the upper deck of the right field grandstand. Babe jogged around the bases with his first home run for the Red Sox. The amazed crowd buzzed with excitement. No one could recall ever seeing a ball hit that far in the Polo Grounds before. In a New York newspaper the next day, a reporter referred to it as a "mighty homer."

The Red Sox lost the game 4–3 in extra innings, but the Babe pitched the entire game and impressed his teammates with his batting and his solid pitching. The game forced Carrigan to see Babe in a new way. The Babe had convinced his manager that he was a superstar in the making and, more importantly, gained confidence in himself. For the remainder of the year, Babe won another seventeen games and lost only once. He finished the season with an 18–8 record and smacked two more home runs for a total of four.

Boston's other pitchers were even better that season and, with an offensive attack led by future Hall of Fame outfielder Tris Speaker, the Red Sox won the pennant and the right to play the Philadelphia Phillies in the World Series. It was the Babe's first World Series and he was thrilled. He couldn't wait to pitch.

The Phillies featured a potent offense led by Gavvy Cravath. Cravath had hit a record twenty-four home runs, many of them into the short porch in left field in the Phillies' home park, the Baker Bowl. The field was so small that a forty-foot wall was built to make it harder to hit home runs out of the portion of the outfield that was only 279 feet from home plate. The big question on everyone's mind was: could the Red Sox's pitching shut Cravath down?

He didn't say it, but Bill Carrigan was wondering the same thing. Most right-handed batters loved left-handed pitching. Cravath was no different. This was often due to the direction of the left-handed pitcher's breaking balls. They break in toward the hitter, making the ball easier to see and therefore easier to hit. Carrigan didn't want a left-handed pitcher to face Cravath in Philadelphia, so Babe was not an option to start. In the first two games, Carrigan pitched Ernie Shore and Rube Foster, his two best right-handers. Apart from a pinch-hitting appearance, Babe sat on the bench as the Sox split the first two games. As he recalled later, "I ate my heart out." To sit and watch the game while being shackled to the bench was the hardest thing that Babe had ever done.

He confronted Carrigan, demanding to know why he wasn't pitching. Carrigan didn't like Babe's "me first" attitude, and when the series shifted to Boston for game three, he passed over the young lefty from Baltimore once again. This time Carrigan pitched left-handed veteran Dutch Leonard. The Red Sox had arranged to play their home games in the more spacious Braves Field, the home of the Boston Braves, rather than in Fenway Park. This was both to seat more fans and to make it harder for Cravath to hit home runs. Dutch Leonard kept Cravath's hits in the ballpark and posted Boston's second win of the series. With Boston up 2–1, Carrigan went back to his two righties. In games four and five, Ernie Shore and Rube Foster pitched Boston to victory, and the Red Sox were crowned the world champions.

The team, and all of Boston, was celebrating, but Babe was heartbroken. Even though he earned more than $3,600 as a member of the winning team, he was crushed that he didn't get to pitch.

That winter, Babe and his wife, Helen, again returned to Baltimore. When he reported for spring training, his teammates and manager hardly recognized him. He had gained twenty pounds during the off-season, and he was much stronger. It was clear that he had been working on his pitching. His fastball was now one of the best in baseball.

However, Boston Red Sox owner Joseph Lannin was having financial trouble. Over the past few seasons he had paid big salaries to keep players from jumping to the Federal League. The Federal League had collapsed during that off-season, and now Lannin wanted to save some money. He sold star outfielder Tris Speaker's contract to Cleveland.

The 1916 Red Sox would have to win or lose with their pitching. Fortunately, Babe Ruth emerged as one of the best pitchers in the league, while periodically showing his potential as a power hitter. Babe had a great season. He won twenty-three games and lost twelve, while leading the league with an earned run average (ERA) of 1.75. Babe had started forty games in 1916—twenty-three of those were complete games and nine were shutouts. He even held the legendary Ty Cobb, who was in his prime, to two hits that season, and pitched three complete-game shutouts against the Detroit Tigers.

The Babe's breakout season paced the Red Sox to a 91–63 record—good enough for first place in the American League. For the second year in a row, the Red Sox won the pennant and were headed to the postseason. Next up: facing the Brooklyn Dodgers in the World Series.

After right-hander Ernie Shore won a tight game one for the Sox, Carrigan tapped Babe to start the second game. Babe was thrilled. After missing out on most of the last postseason, he was determined to make an impression—and to win.

In the first inning, however, Babe got off to a bad start. Brooklyn outfielder Hy Myers hit a line drive to center field. It skipped past the Boston center fielder, who tripped trying to chase the ball, and it rolled to the wall. Myers raced around the bases for an inside-the-park home run. Babe regained his composure, buckled down, and in the third inning knocked in the game-tying run with a ground ball.

Inning after inning, Babe and Brooklyn pitcher Sherry Smith battled, neither giving way nor making a mistake. It was an even matchup to the end, with neither pitcher faltering. The game remained tied at 1–1 as the sun slowly set and the two teams headed to extra innings.

Finally, in the bottom of the fourteenth inning, Boston managed to push across a run and the game was over. Boston won the game 2–1, behind one of the greatest pitching performances in the history of baseball. *The New York Times* called it "the most thrilling world's series battle ever fought." After the first-inning run, Babe had pitched thirteen innings of shutout ball. It is still one of the best performances in World Series history. When the game was over, he gave Bill Carrigan a huge hug and bellowed, "I told you a year ago I could take care of those National League bums, and you never gave me a chance!" Boston went on to win the series in five games and became world champions for the second consecutive year. This time when the city celebrated, so did the Babe.

It was a hectic off-season. The Red Sox owner Joseph Lannin sold the team to Harry Frazee, an extremely successful producer of Broadway plays. Manager Bill Carrigan retired and was replaced by Jack Barry. The year 1917 brought other changes, too. The United States declared war on Germany and became involved in World War I. The government instituted a draft to build up the military. Baseball, like all parts of American life, was thrown into disarray.

Babe himself was also going through some personal turmoil. On the field, he pitched just as well as he had in 1916. But off the field, he began to spin out of control. He was famous now and quite rich. He was earning more than $5,000 a season, which was a lot of money in those days. He still liked to party, and he didn't respect manager Barry as much as he did Carrigan, whom he hadn't listened to much, either. Babe started drinking more and staying out all hours of the night more frequently.

Then his on-field behavior started to spiral as well. On June 23, in a game against the Washington Senators, he became enraged when umpire Brick Owens called his first four pitches balls. As the leadoff hitter jogged to first base on a walk, Babe rushed the plate and confronted Owens. When the umpire told Babe he would throw him from the game if he didn't settle down, the Babe screamed, "Throw me out and I'll punch you in the jaw!" So Owens tossed him from the game—and Babe hit the ump. The blow struck the umpire in the side of the head and knocked him to the ground. Babe received a well-deserved one-week suspension and was fined $100. Fortunately for the Red Sox, Ernie Shore came on in relief and didn't give up a hit the rest of the game.

That season, Babe won twenty-four games, but it was the White Sox who won the pennant, besting Boston by nine games. It was a letdown after making it to the World Series the last two seasons. That off-season, Babe and Helen stayed near Boston on a farm he had purchased and named Home Plate, instead of returning to Baltimore as they had in previous years. Although he enjoyed being on the farm with Helen, the bright lights of Boston proved too enticing for the fun-loving ballplayer. He spent much of his time going out in the city. He loved driving—especially driving fast. Once during that off-season, he narrowly avoided being killed when he crashed his car into a trolley.

Still, when spring training started in 1918, the Babe was there and ready to play his best. Because of the draft and the war, the Red Sox didn't have quite enough players. This was a problem for many baseball teams that season. Even manager Jack Barry had joined the military and was replaced by Ed Barrow. Babe Ruth had spent multiple seasons as a pitcher, but he was so good he could play wherever his manager needed him. So Babe the pitcher became Babe the outfielder, the first baseman, and the slugger. Fans were worried that their best pitcher was being wasted at first base. But then Babe hit several screamers over the Fenway wall, and fans started turning out as much to see him hit as they did to see him pitch.

When the season officially opened, Babe returned to full-time mound duty. In a 5–4 loss to the Yankees on May 4, he slugged a long home run into the upper deck of the Polo Grounds. In the next game, he played first base and hit another long home run. Then he did it again in his next contest, this time off the great Walter Johnson. By May 11, Babe was leading the league in hitting. Over the next few months he was the sensation of the league, hitting four more home runs and pitching quite well.

Babe enjoyed pitching, but he *loved* hitting. Nothing in his life gave him as big a thrill as smashing a long fly ball for a home run and then jogging around the bases while the fans rose to their feet and chanted his name. Babe was already one of the most popular players in the game.

By midsummer, he had hit a league-best eleven home runs and decided he didn't want to pitch anymore. The problem was that the Red Sox had enough hitting. Boston needed him on the mound. Frustrated, Babe refused, and left the team to join a semipro club in Maryland that offered him a big salary. The Red Sox threatened to file a lawsuit to prevent the Babe from playing for another team. His Boston teammates felt betrayed. They liked Babe, but they thought he was selfish for abandoning them midseason. After realizing the Red Sox could take him to court for breaking his contract, Ruth reluctantly returned to the team and took his regular turn in the rotation, making only an occasional appearance on the field as his batting average slumped.

Babe came back just in time to save the season. He won nine of his last eleven starts, and the Red Sox took command of the American League and won the pennant. Despite missing quite a few games, Babe finished the season with a record of 13–7 and a .300 batting average. The Red Sox then faced the Chicago Cubs in the World Series.

The Red Sox started Babe in game one in Chicago. He was magnificent. He put in a nine-inning shift and shut out the Cubs, allowing only six hits, walking one, and striking out four. George White-man, the Red Sox left fielder, was the other big hero of the game, cracking two hits to help Boston score the only run they needed in the 1–0 victory.

The two teams split the next two games and then traveled by train to Boston to continue the series. On the journey back home, Babe started goofing around—running through the train, grabbing straw hats and punching holes in them. Then, just before the train reached Boston, he ran out of straw hats to destroy. Still bubbling with energy, he scuffled with teammate Walt Kinney. Babe took a swing at Kin-ney and accidentally punched the steel wall of the train car with his left hand—his pitching hand.

The Babe howled in pain. His middle knuckle started to swell immediately. Manager Barry was understandably upset. "You fool," he said. "You're supposed to pitch tomorrow!"

Babe knew he'd messed up. He gritted his teeth and said, "I'll be okay. I'll pitch tomorrow."

Sure enough, Babe took the mound for the fourth game of the series. The Babe was as tough as nails. His swollen hand made it difficult for him to grip the ball and he couldn't get the ball to move like he wanted. Without this control, Babe gave up a large number of hits and walks, but still managed to keep the Cubs in check. In the fourth inning, Babe came to bat with two men on base. After working the count to 3–2, he smacked a long drive that came off the bat so fast it slipped just out of reach of the right fielder for a triple. As one newspaper reporter put it, the hit made "a sound like rifle shot [that] echoed through the park." The hit drove in two runs and the Red Sox led 2–0 until the eighth inning.

With his injured hand forcing Babe to work harder, he tired more quickly than he normally would. In the eighth inning, the Cubs jumped on Babe's mistakes and tagged him for two runs to tie the game. Few people realized it at the time, but these two runs ended an unbelievable streak. Babe had pitched 29 and ⅔ consecutive scoreless innings in the World Series, a new record that would stand for another forty-two years until broken by Yankees pitcher Whitey Ford, who would go 33 innings without giving up a run.

In the bottom of the eighth, pinch hitter Wally Schang got on base with a single, and right fielder Harry Hooper managed to sacrifice-bunt the go-ahead across the plate. Babe started the ninth, but Barry could tell Babe was done. The manager quickly called on his bullpen to bring in Bullet Joe Bush to finish the game off, and Babe went into left field for the Red Sox. They closed down the game and had all the momentum on their side.

Up three games to one, the Sox put in a poor performance in game five before squeaking out a win in game six to win the series, their third World Series

Transcendental Graphics / contributor / Getty Images

BABE WARMS UP TO PITCH BEFORE A 1916 GAME IN FENWAY PARK.

championship in four years. Babe had won his two starts, but apart from a late appearance in the outfield in the final game, he sat on the bench for the rest of the series.

It had been an incredible year for the Babe, and one that was never to be repeated. No one knew it yet, but Babe Ruth's career as a pitcher—and as a member of the Boston Red Sox—was just about over.

CHAPTER FOUR
1919–1923

BECOMING THE BAMBINO

On November 11, 1918, World War I ended and baseball returned to normal. Most of the players the Red Sox had lost during the war rejoined the team. The defending champions looked even stronger than before.

Because of his stellar season the previous year, Babe felt he deserved more money. The trouble was, he already had a contract for $7,000 a year. When Harry Frazee refused to raise his salary, Babe held out, refusing to play in 1919 unless he received a big raise. Spring training had already started when Frazee gave in and signed Babe to a new three-year contract worth $10,000 per season. It was one of the biggest contracts in baseball.

Babe reported to camp in Tampa, Florida, and immediately got everyone's attention. In the off-season Babe had come to a decision. Even though he was one of the best hurlers in baseball, he didn't want to pitch anymore. He just wanted to hit. So the first time he took the field, in an exhibition game against the New York Giants, he played the outfield.

He came to bat in the second inning. The pitcher threw the ball and Babe took a huge cut at it— *boom!* The bat connected with the ball and made an unmistakable sound. It was like a cannon, or a firecracker, or a shotgun. In a heartbeat the ball exploded over the right fielder's head and just kept going. By the time the outfielder hopped over the short fence and retrieved the ball, Babe had reached home plate. After the game, several people attempted to measure how far the home run had traveled. According to some accounts, the ball traveled an amazing six hundred feet!

When the Red Sox opened the season a few weeks later, Babe was still in the outfield. In less than a week, he found himself in big trouble. While the Red Sox played in Washington, Babe stayed out all night. A hotel worker woke manager Ed Barrow when Babe returned at six in the morning. The manager knocked on Babe's door. Babe, still dressed and smoking a pipe, quickly jumped under the covers, pulled them up to his neck, and told the manager to come in.

Barrow stormed into the room, walked over to the bed, and snatched the covers from Babe. Barrow could see that he was still in his clothes. He gave Babe a disgusted look and barked, "I'll see you at the ballpark!" Later that day, Barrow suspended Babe for a day and gave him a piece of advice: "Turn your life around."

For a while, Babe heeded the advice, at least off the field. On the field, however, he struggled. Once the season started, his big bat was silent and the move to the outfield seemed like a big mistake. By the first of June, he was one of the worst hitters in the league. The Red Sox weren't scoring runs with Babe in the lineup, and they sorely missed him on the pitching mound. The World Series champs were already out of the pennant race, their season effectively over.

Barrow and Frazee begged Babe to return to the mound. He reluctantly agreed, but only if he was still allowed to play the outfield between starts. Almost immediately his bat perked up and he started hitting home runs at a record rate. It was too late to help the Sox that season, but fans began to turn out in droves to see him hit, particularly in

New York, where for some reason he always hit the ball better than anywhere else.

Babe loved the attention and stayed hot for the rest of the season, breaking Gavvy Cravath's record with twenty-nine home runs. He helped out on the mound occasionally, too, but the turnaround came too late for the Red Sox. They finished in sixth place.

Then Babe made another huge mistake. Just a few days before the end of the season, he left without permission to play an exhibition game for extra money. He had again put himself and his needs in front of the team, instead of acting like the leader he should have been. That angered his teammates, manager Barrow, and owner Frazee.

Over the past few seasons, Frazee had been fighting with Ban Johnson, the president of the American League. Johnson didn't want Frazee to own the Red Sox anymore, and Frazee didn't think Johnson should be league president. The other teams took sides, with the Red Sox, Yankees, and White Sox battling Johnson in the courts over a variety of issues.

In the midst of all this trouble, Frazee didn't need more aggravation from his players. In the last few years, Babe had put himself above the team, running around at all hours of the night, not taking care of himself, and not thinking about what was best for the Red Sox. He was a great player, there was no doubt of that, but he had also become a huge headache. When Babe demanded yet another raise and a new contract, Frazee decided he had had enough. He knew Babe was a popular and talented player whom many clubs would be interested in acquiring. He decided to sell Babe Ruth's contract while the price was high, and rebuild.

The New York Yankees needed a star attraction. Since joining the American League in 1903, they had never won a pennant. But in 1919, new owners Jacob Ruppert and Cap Huston had money to spend. They decided to build the team around Babe Ruth, as a hitter, not a pitcher.

Frazee held out until Ruppert and Huston offered over $100,000 for Babe's contract. Just before the New Year, Frazee agreed to sell the great Babe Ruth to the Yankees.

Some fans and sportswriters in Boston were furious about the sale. They believed that Frazee had given away their best player. Others agreed with Frazee, who said "the Yankees are taking quite a risk" with Babe. In New York, some thought Babe would become a star and lead the Yankees to a pennant. Others worried that he was too out of control and that he might never again hit as well as he had in 1918. The sale was a gamble on both sides.

Babe played to the press in both cities. In Boston, he told reporters he hated to leave, and he told the reporters in New York he was thrilled to be a Yankee. That thrill was made even sweeter when the Yankees gave him a new contract worth $20,000 per year in 1921 and 1922.

Baseball was going through some changes in Babe's first few years as a Yankee. In August of 1920, a player named Ray Chapman was struck in the head by a pitch and died in a hospital twelve hours later. After Chapman's untimely death, major league baseball instigated some new rules about pitching. Spitballs were made illegal, for one thing. For another, new baseballs had to be used whenever the one in play became discolored, scratched, scuffed, or incurred any damage. The new balls were harder, brighter, and easier to see. This made them easier to hit for home runs. For home run hitters like Babe, the new balls were great news.

The park where the Yankees played, the Polo

Grounds, was also tailor-made for a pull hitter like Babe. The right-field fence was much closer than the one in Fenway Park. Although Babe would have undoubtedly hit plenty of home runs if he had stayed in Boston, he never would have set the records he set at the Polo Grounds.

Baseball needed a hero. It was a dark time for the league. Along with teams fighting the American League about leadership and policy issues, and the first death in the game's history, the league was also reeling from the recent "Black Sox" scandal. Rumors were swirling that in 1919 the Chicago White Sox had thrown the World Series. Although it would take nearly a year before the scope of the plot was fully known, baseball was in desperate need of a lovable star to regain the fans' trust. Babe Ruth was ready-made for the role.

No transition is easy, and Babe got off to a rocky start with the Yankees. Although he hit well in the spring, his behavior raised many eyebrows. In the middle of one exhibition game, he went into the stands and tried to attack a fan who had been teasing him. He caused problems for management, too. He insisted on playing center field. When manager Miller Huggins resisted, Babe went over his head to make his case with the Yankee owners. They agreed, although Babe settled into right field eventually.

All eyes were on the newest Yankee as the season began in 1920. On opening day, Babe lost his focus and misplayed a fly ball, costing his team a road win. In his second game, he struck out three times. Then the Yankees played the Red Sox in Boston. Babe did nothing. The Red Sox swept New York. Babe was looking like a big bust. The reporters in New York started to question the decision to bring in a player whose best days were behind him.

Things didn't improve when the Yankees played their first home game. Babe swung too hard at a pitch in batting practice and separated his ribs. After that, swinging a bat was painful for him and he struck out repeatedly. By May 1, the Yankees were only 4–7. Meanwhile, the Red Sox were in first place—without the Babe.

When Babe's ribs finally healed, he started to hit. His first home run as a Yankee, a long blast at the Polo Grounds, seemed to shake him loose. For the rest of the season, he blasted home run after home run after home run, to the fans' delight. By mid-season, New York surged into first place. On July 15, Babe broke his own home run record when he smacked his thirtieth round-tripper of the season. Every home run he hit for the remainder of the season only added to the record.

Baseball fans finally had something to cheer for and were packing stadiums wherever the Yankees played. They may not all have been Yankee fans, but they were all Babe Ruth fans.

There was something about the Babe that fans found irresistible. He did everything in a big way. Even his strikeouts were exciting, as the momentum of his swing still nearly knocked him to the ground every time he missed. Babe knew how to play to the crowd, and fans were thrilled when he tipped his cap and revealed his smiling, moon-shaped face after hitting a home run, or grimaced after missing a pitch, or bellowed a complaint to an umpire.

With his new popularity came new nicknames. Many of the fans following the games locally were Italian and they christened him "Bambino," which is Italian for "baby" or "babe." New York sportswriters also used nicknames when describing him, such as the "Colossus of Clout," the "Mauling Monarch," the "Prince of Pounders," and the "Sultan of Swat." They wrote about him every day throughout the season. Every home run he hit was news, and so was every strikeout.

For all his home run hitting, record breaking, and new national popularity, the Babe couldn't salvage the Yankees' season. In August, Yankees pitcher Carl Mays accidentally hit Cleveland Indians shortstop Ray Chapman in the head with a pitch. Chapman died as a result of his injuries and, after the tragedy, the Indians rallied around the memory of their fallen teammate to take the pennant.

Babe finished the season with a batting average of .376 and a record fifty-four home runs. His home run total that season was higher than that of almost every team in baseball—only two teams managed to hit as many home runs among all their players as Babe Ruth was able to hit by himself. There seemed to be no limit to what he could accomplish. Fans wondered if he would one day hit sixty or even seventy home runs in a season.

His performance transformed the game forever. After seeing what Babe could accomplish, other players changed their approach at the plate. Instead of just trying to make contact, more hitters began to swing from their heels like Babe Ruth. Before him, most batters hit home runs by accident. Now they tried to imitate the Babe. In the year following Babe's record run, the home run would become more common.

Babe quickly cashed in on his fame. He starred in a movie called *Headin' Home* and endorsed all sorts of products, from Girl Scout cookies to soap. He had a sports column written under his name by sportswriter Christy Walsh. He also went on a long "barnstorming" trip, playing a series of exhibition games after the season and hitting home runs against local teams before thousands of fans. Although organized baseball considered such tours illegal, Babe didn't care. He had become the most famous man in America, and he was making more money off the field than on it.

Of course, having lots of cash made it even more difficult for him to stay out of trouble. A new amendment to the Constitution in 1919 had made the sale of alcohol illegal and ushered in an era known as Prohibition. Even that didn't slow down the Babe. He spent a lot of his time in what were known as "speakeasies," illegal underground bars and taverns that served alcohol. Life in the off-season was one big party. When he turned up for spring training, he had packed on the pounds and was much heavier than he had been the year before.

It was a struggle for Babe to get in shape that spring, but when he did, he rapidly resumed his record hitting in 1921. Pitchers were afraid of him and rarely gave him a good pitch to hit. When they did, he knocked it out of the park.

Babe and the Yankees took the American League by storm. At the end of the season, he had increased his home run record to an incredible fifty-nine. The Yankees won the pennant, but they would have to get through their rivals the New York Giants in the World Series.

The Giants, led by feisty manager John McGraw, were a terrific team that season. They still played baseball the old-fashioned way, scratching and clawing for runs with bunts, base hits, and stolen bases. McGraw, considered the best manager in baseball at the time, promised everyone that his pitchers would shut down the Bambino and the Yankees—a promise he made good on.

This was a unique series, because both the Yankees and the Giants played their home games at the Polo Grounds. That meant that neither team would have home-field advantage for their home games.

The stadium would be packed with hordes of both teams' fans.

In a sense, the Yankees lost the series in the second game. After winning game one, the Yankees also took game two. But in the middle of the game, Babe slid roughly into third base after already drawing three walks. As he twisted away from being tagged, he scraped his elbow.

At first Babe shrugged off the injury. But in game three, a game in which the Giants drubbed the Yankees 13–5, he scraped it again. The hope was that some rest would help the elbow, but there wasn't much time between games. By game four, Babe could barely move his arm because the elbow was infected, badly swollen, and very red. He struck out three times, collecting his only hit on a bunt. By then it was obvious he couldn't continue to play because of the pain. For the rest of the series, he made only one appearance, as a pinch hitter.

Without the Bambino, the Yankees were an average team. The Giants stormed back to win the best-of-nine series five games to three. Despite his record fifty-nine regular-season home runs, 1921 ended in disappointment for Babe.

After the season, baseball commissioner Kenesaw Mountain Landis warned Babe not to go on another illegal barnstorming tour. Babe ignored him and went anyway. He felt as if he were bigger than the game.

He wasn't. In December, Landis suspended him for the first six weeks of the 1922 season.

Fortunately, the Yankees had earned so much money from the previous season's World Series run that they were able to acquire a number of other valuable players, many from the Red Sox. Although they missed Babe at the start of the season and sometimes struggled even after his return, the Yankees still had enough firepower and pitching to win the pennant.

However, Babe was in a slump, at least for him. His batting average dropped to .315 and he hit *only* thirty-five home runs, not enough to beat the new league leader, Ken Williams of the St. Louis Browns, who hit thirty-nine.

Meanwhile, Babe's behavior off the field was a major distraction once again. When he returned to the team after the suspension, he was out of shape and never really got going. As the season progressed, he spent night after night out on the town and often showed up at the ballpark bleary-eyed and disheveled. One of his Yankee roommates later said he didn't really room with Babe, he roomed "with his suitcase," because Babe was always out. On the field, Babe argued with umpires and was suspended several times for using bad language. Nobody, not even Yankees manager Huggins, was able to control Babe.

The Yankees met the Giants in the World Series for the second season in a row. This time, it wasn't even close. The Giants won it all in five games and Babe was terrible, collecting only two hits.

At a banquet Babe attended shortly after the end of the series, speaker after speaker lectured him about his behavior and the way in which he had disappointed not only his teammates but also the fans and the city of New York. New York state senator Jimmy Walker said, "You have let down the kids of America.... They have seen their idol shattered and their dream broken." Babe was humiliated and told everyone, "I'm going back to my farm to get in shape."

His career was at a crossroads, and he knew it. If

he didn't do something fast, he wouldn't be Babe Ruth anymore. This time, he didn't have anyone like Brother Matthias to bail him out. Babe would have to help himself. It was time for him to grow up—at least a little.

CHAPTER FIVE
1923

THE FIRST OF TWENTY-SEVEN TITLES

Babe Ruth kept his promise that winter. He returned to his Massachusetts farm, reuniting with Helen after a long separation, and rarely ventured into the city. He stopped drinking, watched what he ate, and spent the winter doing farmwork, skating, chopping wood, and going for long hikes. He knew he had messed up in 1922 and was determined to prove that he was still the best player in the game.

New York fans were looking forward to the 1923 season. At the cost of $2.5 million, the Yankees had finally built their own ballpark. Now the Yankees would play in Yankee Stadium, no longer guests at the Polo Grounds, home of the Giants. The new park in the Bronx was huge and capable of holding more than 70,000 fans. Most of the fans were looking forward to seeing the Babe hit some home runs in his new home. The park designers had done what they could to satisfy the fans, making sure the fence in right field was short enough for Babe to hit home runs with the same frequency he had at the Polo Grounds.

That year, the Bambino didn't let them down. He showed up at spring training in tremendous shape. He had shed his extra weight and arrived at camp a slender 209 pounds.

On opening day at Yankee Stadium, the Babe announced his return in dramatic fashion. With the Yankees up 1–0 in the fourth inning, the Sultan of Swat came to bat. Boston pitcher Howard Ehmke let a ball over the plate and Babe knocked the stuffing out of it. The ball soared deep and high over the right-field wall as everyone in the stadium stood and craned their necks to watch the flight of the ball. When it finally came back to earth, it was ten rows deep in the right-field stands. Babe Ruth was the first player to hit a home run in Yankee Stadium! After that day, a sportswriter referred to the stadium as "the House that Ruth Built," a nickname that stayed with the beautiful ballpark until Yankee Stadium was torn down in 2010.

For the rest of the season, there was no stopping the Yankees. Although Babe didn't hit home runs quite like the last few seasons (he ended the season with only forty-one), he did hit better than ever. For most of the season, Babe's average hovered above .400, and though he finished with a .393 batting average, it was still the second best in the league. The Yankees won the pennant by sixteen games over Detroit. Once again, they played the New York Giants in the World Series.

Thus far, Babe had done everything in New York but help the Yankees win a championship. For all his accomplishments, he knew he wouldn't really be considered a success until the Yankees won the series. In the end, the Babe knew that you were remembered for the titles you won more than anything else. Giants manager John McGraw entered the series confident that he had the Yankees' number. After all, his pitchers had shut down Babe in the last two World Series by throwing him outside curveballs.

"The same system will suffice," McGraw said before the series began.

This time, however, Babe had a plan of his own. He tripled in the first game and the Yankees lost, but in game two he broke loose with two long home runs and narrowly missed a third. The series was tied at a game apiece. The Giants went on to win the third game of the series 1–0 on a Casey Stengel inside-the-park home run. During the game, the Giants chose to walk Babe twice rather than let him hit. McGraw's system would not suffice. In fact, McGraw was scratching his head, trying to figure out how to stop Babe's bat. Over the next two games, the Yankees outscored the Giants 16 to 5. They won the next two games to finally take the series away from their crosstown rivals. It was the best payback a team could ask for.

Yankees owner Jacob Ruppert was ecstatic. "Now I have the greatest ballpark and the greatest team," he said. Everyone already knew he had the greatest player—Babe Ruth.

For New York fans over the centuries, for the city as a whole, the 1923 World Series represented something greater than a championship. That championship was the start of an entire dynasty, the first of what would be twenty-seven titles for the Yankees—more titles than any other team in major league baseball history.

CHAPTER SIX
1924–1925

IT ALL CATCHES UP WITH YOU

The following year, the cocky Yankees figured they'd win another world championship just by showing up. Although the Babe had started drifting back to his old ways and was again gaining weight, most observers figured the Yankees still had more than enough firepower and pitching to win.

But the overconfident Yankees got off to a slow start. Before the season, they foolishly released pitcher Carl Mays. He later won twenty games for Cincinnati, while the Yankees' pitching staff fell apart. By midseason the Yankees were battling Washington and Detroit for the pennant.

Babe was having another great year, just a shade below his performance in 1923. Still, despite cracking forty-six home runs and hitting .378, he couldn't put the Yankees over the top. They finished second in the American League and missed out on the World Series for the first time in four years.

Unlike the previous winter, Babe didn't take care of himself over the break. Instead of spending the off-season on his farm, getting ready for a fresh start in the new season, he ran all over the country eating, drinking, and partying the night away. By the time he started thinking about the upcoming season, he weighed nearly 260 pounds! He tried to lose weight, but when spring training began, he was still overweight, drinking heavily, and staying up all hours of the night.

Manager Miller Huggins repeatedly cautioned Babe about his behavior, but the Bambino just laughed at him. Huggins was a little man and Babe didn't take him seriously. Besides, despite being out of shape, he hit nearly .500 during spring training. He felt indestructible, but he wasn't.

Near the end of spring training, all the late nights, drinking binges, smoking, and overeating caught up with him. The Yankees were on their way back to New York when Babe, who had been complaining of stomach cramps, collapsed on a train platform in North Carolina.

Rumors swept the country that he had died, but after a few days he felt a little better and left with Yankees scout Paul Krichell to rejoin the team. He made it as far as Washington, DC, before collapsing again. This time he fell unconscious.

Krichell somehow got Babe on the train to New York. When the train pulled into the station, he had to be removed through a window onto a stretcher. The Babe couldn't walk and was so heavy that the stretcher could not be maneuvered down the aisle. He was rushed to St. Vincent's Hospital and admitted on April 9. He remained in the hospital for the next six weeks.

Over time, the illness became known as the "bellyache heard around the world," and it was often blamed on too many hot dogs and too much soda pop. But that wasn't the cause. Babe was seriously ill. Although the exact nature of the illness was a mystery, he did undergo a minor operation to remove an intestinal abscess. Some have speculated that he was embarrassed by a disease, while others believe Babe may have been receiving treatment for alcoholism. Whatever the cause, he was very, very sick for a long time.

When he finally left the hospital on May 26, he didn't look like Babe Ruth. He had lost thirty pounds, and his legs were rail thin and shaky from lack of exercise. His gaunt face made him look

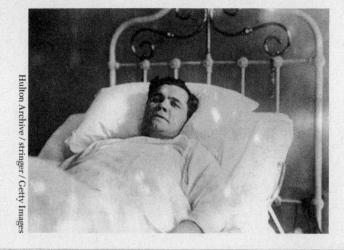

Hulton Archive / stringer / Getty Images

BABE LYING IN HIS HOSPITAL BED DURING HIS RECOVERY

twenty years older. Even when he felt well enough to play again, he didn't play like Babe Ruth.

The Yankees had struggled without him and were already out of the pennant race. Through June and July, Babe hit only .250 with a handful of home runs. The one bright spot on the team was rookie first baseman Lou Gehrig, who was hitting nearly .300.

New York sportswriters looked at Babe and saw a player near the end of his career. He was a thirty-year-old man who looked like he was fifty. Despite his weight loss in the hospital, he was still too heavy and waddled around the bases. A hard run left him weak. Pitchers weren't afraid of him anymore. On one occasion Huggins even removed Babe from a game for a pinch hitter.

Incredibly, within weeks of leaving the hospital, Babe resumed his late-night lifestyle. That didn't help his recovery. He had met another woman, Claire Hodgson, and wanted to marry her, but he couldn't divorce Helen. On and off the field, Babe was a mess.

It all came to a head on August 29 in St. Louis. Babe stayed out past team curfew and got caught. When he arrived at the park the next day, Miller Huggins told him, "Don't bother getting dressed. I'm suspending you and fining you $5,000. You're to go back to New York."

"What?" Babe bellowed. He couldn't believe Huggins would do that, but the manager had already checked with Jacob Ruppert and the owner told him to do what he felt was best for the team.

"If you were half my size I'd punch you," Babe said.

Huggins stood his ground and didn't flinch.

"If I were half your size, I'd punch *you*," he replied.

Then he told Babe not to return to the ball club until he was ready to apologize, not only to Huggins, but also to his teammates.

Babe was angry and hurt. He railed against Huggins to the press and said he was going to appeal to commissioner Landis or to Ruppert. He didn't like when people told him what to do. After all, he was Babe Ruth. He foolishly believed that because he was so popular and famous, either Landis or Ruppert would order Huggins to put him back in the lineup. Ruth told the press he expected Landis to "do the right thing," and that Huggins "has Ruppert buffaloed. Huggins is trying to make me the goat." Babe wanted Huggins fired and said he would never play for him again. If the suspension was upheld, Babe said he was prepared to quit the game.

But Babe misread both Landis and Ruppert. Landis didn't even want to meet with him and announced that he supported the suspension. Ruppert was even more direct, saying, "I understand Ruth says he will not play for the Yankees as long as Huggins is manager. Well, Huggins will be manager as long as he wants to be."

Babe was shocked.

Everyone liked Babe. Everyone wanted to see

him play, but they also all agreed that unless he started taking care of himself and changed his ways, the Yankees were better off without him. No one was bigger than the game.

After a few days, Babe asked Huggins if he could apologize and the manager turned him down. He wanted Babe to fully understand how serious the situation was. As Babe waited on the sideline, he began to realize how much he enjoyed playing and how he was wasting his life. He even called Brother Matthias and spent several hours discussing his future.

Finally, after nine long days, Huggins agreed to meet Babe. The Sultan of Swat approached his manager like an ashamed little boy and apologized profusely. Then Huggins told him he would have to make the same apology to his teammates. The Yankees gathered in the clubhouse and Babe sheepishly entered the room, nearly in tears.

"I was wrong," he admitted. "I'm too hotheaded."

He knew he had let everyone down. More importantly, he had let himself down and wasted his talents, while ruining the season for his team and the fans.

Babe was allowed to rejoin the team, but the

season could not be saved. The Yankees finished seventh and he hit only .290, with twenty-five home runs. Babe had always enjoyed the backing of the press, but his behavior had turned even the sportswriters against him. Many believed he should retire and that the Yankees would be better off without him.

Despite hitting all the home runs, Babe had yet to fulfill his promise as a Yankee. While they had won three pennants, they had won only one world championship, and in the seasons after that Babe had done little to excite New York's management, his teammates, or the fans. Unless he permanently turned his life around, his career as a Yankee would be a failure.

CHAPTER SEVEN
1926–1928

THE GREATEST

The suspension forced Babe Ruth into taking his life and his baseball career seriously. He separated from Helen, and she moved from the farm back to Boston. He felt badly about his marriage falling apart, but he knew he had hardly been the ideal husband. All winter long he'd tried to make amends for his horrible performance in 1925, but it was too little too late.

He turned down a chance to make money on another exhibition tour. He wrote a magazine article in which he apologized to the fans and admitted he had acted like "a boob." Determined to get back in shape, he put his fitness in the hands of gym owner Artie McGovern.

It helped that he had the love and support of Claire Hodgson. Babe respected her opinion the way he did Brother Matthias's. When she told Babe he had to change, he listened. He realized that if he did not, he would lose more than his baseball career. He might also lose her.

Every day, he spent four hours at the gym working out. At first, the exercise sessions, weightlifting, handball, long walks, and steam baths left him exhausted. But ever so slowly, he began to lose weight and replace flab with muscle. He transformed himself from the soft Babe of the previous seasons to an athlete cast in iron.

By February of 1926, he was ready to play again. He had lost nearly thirty pounds and almost ten inches from his waist. Although no one would ever accuse Babe of being slender, he was once again a powerful athlete.

Meanwhile, the Yankees had added infielder Tony Lazzeri, who was a terrific hitter. Lou Gehrig was beginning to show signs of being as dangerous at the plate as Babe. Claire stayed close to Babe, and she kept him from running around at all hours of the night.

The Yankees got off to a great start and kept on going. Babe Ruth wasn't just back—he was all the way back. Babe hit .372 and smashed 47 home runs while driving in 155 runs. Lazzeri and Gehrig each knocked in over a hundred runs as well, and the Yankees cruised to the pennant. Their matchup for that World Series was the St. Louis Cardinals. It would not be an easy series for the Yankees.

The Yankees were big favorites, but the Cardinals were a talented team. After New York won the first game, the Cardinals came back to win the next two. Babe was mired in a postseason slump. He had collected only two singles in the first three games. Game four in St. Louis was a must-win for New York.

Babe came to the plate determined to do whatever it took to give his team that win. In the first inning, he hit the first pitch he saw for a home run. In the third inning, he hit another home run. Then, in the sixth inning, he truly outdid himself.

Sitting on a full count, Babe took a swing at a ball hanging over the plate and hit it harder than he had ever hit a ball before. It soared deep to center field. Once it started it just kept going and going. Announcer Graham McNamee was broadcasting the game to the nation over the radio. Fans all over the country were glued to their radios waiting for Babe to do something special, and this was the moment.

> *The Babe hits it into the center-field bleachers for a home run! A home run! Did you hear what I said? Oh, what a shot!...This is a World Series record, three home runs in one series game....They tell me that's the first ball ever hit into the center-field stand. That's a mile and a half from here!*

It wasn't quite that far, but it was the farthest ball ever hit in St. Louis. Even Cardinal fans stood and applauded the Babe. It was in fact the first ball ever hit into the center-field bleachers. Not that the ball stopped there—it bounced out of the bleachers into the street!

No one knew, however, that the home run meant even more to a little boy listening to McNamee's broadcast. Young Johnny Sylvester had been badly hurt in a fall from a horse and was laid up in a New York hospital. His father had asked for the Cardinals and Yankees to send him some autographed baseballs to cheer his son up. The teams did, and Babe added a promise that he would hit a home run for Johnny. The boy heard McNamee's call on all three of Babe's home runs. A smile spread across Johnny Sylvester's face that didn't go away for days.

The Yankees crushed the Cardinals by a score of 10–5. They took the next game, thanks to a great save made by the Babe. The Yankees were up in the series, but the Cardinals fought back and took game six to force a final game.

It came down to the last game, and ultimately, the final pitch. The Yankees had played a great game, but the Cardinals played better. In the ninth the Yankees trailed 3–2. With two out, Babe drew a walk. If he could get to home plate, the Yankees would tie the game. Yankees outfielder Bob Meusel dug in at the plate. Suddenly, Babe took off and tried to steal second! The throw from home came in fast, hard, and on target. Babe was out by a mile—and so were the Yankees.

Babe was roundly criticized for the play. It dampened an otherwise great series and a great comeback for the Babe.

The loss only made Babe and the Yankees more

determined to win it all in 1927. Babe had proven to his teammates that he was in control of his life, so no one worried anymore about his off-the-field distractions. Although he still liked to have fun and still had an enormous appetite, he knew when to stop and made sure that he was ready to play every day.

And that is exactly what he did. No one will ever forget Babe Ruth and the 1927 Yankees.

Everything went right. Many people still consider the 1927 Yankees to be the greatest team in the history of baseball. They had great pitching, great fielding, and great hitting. They didn't just beat other teams—they beat them badly. One of the main reasons was the emergence of Lou Gehrig.

The very first time a Yankees scout saw Gehrig playing for Columbia University, he called him "another Ruth." Now in his third season in the major leagues, Gehrig was about to prove that scout right. Gehrig hit fourth in the Yankees lineup, right behind Babe. Together, the two Yankees stars formed the greatest slugging duo in the history of baseball. Sportswriters dubbed the lineup "Murderers' Row."

From the start of the season, Babe and Gehrig sent shivers down the backs of American League pitchers. It seemed as if one of them hit one or two home runs every day. The Yankees scored runs in by the handful.

One opposing pitcher admitted, "I would rather pitch a doubleheader against any other club than a single game against the Yankees."

Babe seemed reinvigorated. Every home run hit by Gehrig seemed to bring out the inner Bambino in Babe Ruth. After all, he had won the major league home run crown in six of the past eight seasons. He didn't want to lose his title to his own teammate. It just proves what a little bit of competition can do for a career.

By midseason, the Yankees were miles ahead of everyone in the pennant race. The big question became who would lead the league in home runs. It was going to be either Babe or Lou Gehrig, and whoever won would most likely break Babe's standing record of fifty-nine home runs.

Entering September, Babe's forty-three home runs were two up on Gehrig. By September 6, both men were stuck on forty-four homers. Then Babe pulled away. The Yankees split the doubleheader against the Red Sox and Babe cracked three home runs, including one fans continue to claim was the longest ever hit at Fenway Park at the time. Then the next day, he hit two more. That pulled Babe within ten home runs of the record.

Over the final weeks of the season, fans all over the country kept track of Babe's home run count. Babe knew everyone was watching, so he responded with remarkable performance after remarkable performance.

On September 22, Babe hit his fifty-sixth home run. It happened in the ninth inning and led the Yankees to their 105th win of the season, tying a mark set by the 1912 Boston Red Sox. As he rounded the bases off the game-winning blast, dozens of fans poured onto the field and ran with him. Some of them tried to take his bat, but Babe held it high over his head, laughing and dashing between his fans on his way to home plate. The record seemed within his grasp.

Over the next week, Babe hit only one more homer. With three games left in the season, the record seemed out of reach. It would take what sportswriters called a "Ruthian" performance to hit sixty home runs. Of course, no one was more Ruthian than Babe Ruth himself.

On September 29, Babe unleashed two home runs to tie the record. After hitting number fifty-nine, he shook Lou Gehrig's hand at home plate and then tipped his hat to the crowd. Even Gehrig, who had stalled at "only" forty-seven home runs, stood in awe of the Babe.

Babe had two more games to hit sixty and break his own record.

The next day, the Yankees played the Washington Senators. In the eighth, they were tied at

Transcendental Graphics / contributor / Getty Images

BABE IS GREETED BY LOU GEHRIG AS HE CROSSES HOME PLATE AFTER HITTING A HOME RUN IN 1929.

two. Although Babe collected two hits and scored both of the Yankees' runs, he couldn't hit the long ball. The last one was definitely going to be the hardest.

With one out, Yankees shortstop Mark Koenig tripled. Babe stepped to the plate. He took a ball on the first pitch and then a strike. Senators pitcher Tom Zachary threw a big, juicy pitch. The ball was low and inside. Babe swung down on the pitch and drove it like a golf ball. The drive sailed to right field, curving toward the line. The umpire tracked the ball to make the call as Babe started a slow dance toward first.

The ball rattled into the seats, but nobody could tell if it had squeaked fair or if it was a foul ball. The umpire stared at the foul pole and the crowd held their breath—then he signaled for fair ball. He twirled his arm above his head, the signal that the hit was a home run. Yankee Stadium exploded with cheers. Babe ran around the bases slowly and deliberately, making sure he touched each base and savoring the moment. The hit gave the Yankees a 4–2 lead and they hung on through the last inning to win the game.

Babe was mobbed by reporters in the clubhouse.

He couldn't stop smiling. Only two years before, many had thought his career was over. Now he had done something no one else had ever done in the history of the game.

"Sixty!" he yelled. "Count 'em, sixty! Let's see someone else do that!" Then a reporter asked him if he thought he would break his own record in 1928. "I don't know and I don't care," he replied with a laugh.

As wonderful as hitting sixty was, Babe knew that the Yankees needed to win the World Series to make the record truly meaningful. If the Yankees lost the series, everyone would say he had still failed.

The National League champion Pittsburgh Pirates were a good team built around brothers and high-average hitters Paul and Lloyd Waner. Before the first game, Babe looked at them and quipped, "Why, they're no bigger than a couple of little kids. If I was that size I'd be afraid of getting hurt."

The 1927 Yankees were a machine. They beat the Pirates 5–4 in the first game and 6–2 in the second. In game three, Babe blasted his first home run of the series, leading his team to an 8–1 victory. He hit another blast in game four to give the Yankees a 3–1 lead, but the Pirates rallied to tie the game 3–3. Then in the ninth inning, New York loaded the bases. The Pirates pitcher uncorked a wild pitch and Yankees outfielder Earle Combs jogged home with the winning run. Combs hadn't broken a sweat, and neither did the Yankees in sweeping the Pirates. For the second time as a Yankee, Babe was a world champion.

That team may have been the best Yankees team ever. Babe and Gehrig hit 214 extra-base hits. Babe hit a record 60 home runs, and added 164 RBIs and 158 runs scored. The team batted .307 and scored a total of 975 runs. From top to bottom, the 1927 World Series champion Yankees were an amazing team.

When the 1928 season began, New York let every other team know that they were still the champs by winning thirty-four of their first forty-two games. Although Babe didn't break his home run record, he did come close by slamming fifty-four home runs. The Yankees won the pennant once again and prepared to face the Cardinals.

It looked as if the Cardinals would have the edge over the Yankees. After their great start, New York didn't play very well over the last half of the season.

Several New York players would miss the World Series with injuries, and Babe was bothered by a bad knee.

But it seems that no one bothered to tell the Yankees they were considered the underdogs. They surged forward to sweep St. Louis in four straight games. Once again, Babe Ruth was the big story. He ended the series with perhaps the greatest day of his career.

Babe wasn't exactly invisible in the first three games, though. Although Lou Gehrig gathered the headlines with three long home runs, Babe collected three hits in game one, two more in game two, and made the play of the game in the third contest, scoring the go-ahead run with a hustle play by dashing home on a ground ball and knocking the ball out of the catcher's glove.

In game four, the legendary player turned in a truly legendary performance. Babe started out on a low note, dropping an easy fly ball in the first inning. When he came to bat in the fourth inning, St. Louis led 1–0. With the swing of his bat, Babe changed the entire game. *Whack!* The game was tied.

Then St. Louis went up by one again. The score was still 2–1 when Babe came to bat in the seventh inning. Up two strikes, the St. Louis pitcher tried an illegal quick pitch. The umpire refused to allow it. Babe then calmly sent the next offering out of the ballpark. As the St. Louis crowd booed, Babe laughed his way around the bases, waving at them. Gehrig followed with a home run to put the Yankees ahead.

When Babe next took the field, St. Louis fans booed him again. Some threw soda bottles at him. Babe picked one up, wound up, and pretended to throw it back. Many fans ducked, but others just laughed as Babe harmlessly tossed the bottle aside. And just like that, he'd won back the crowd. Miraculously, even the Cardinals fans were on his side.

Babe came up once more in the eighth and put the game away with another home run, his third of the game. But he wasn't done yet.

With two out in the ninth, the Cardinals were down to their last at bat. A St. Louis batter hit a towering fly ball down the line. Babe took off running at full speed. Fans in the stands threw paper to try to distract him. It didn't work. Babe was running a dead sprint when he jumped into the stands and snagged the ball without breaking stride. He held it over his head, whooping, "There's the ball! The one that says it's all over!"

For the Cardinals, it was. The Yankees were champions again.

Babe Ruth was at his peak. The Yankees had won three straight pennants and two World Series since he'd taken control of his life. He was more beloved than ever.

CHAPTER EIGHT
1929–1932

THE CALLED SHOT?

The last three seasons had been the best of Babe's career, and the happiest. He was again the greatest player in the game, and the Yankees were the greatest team in baseball. But the next few seasons would not be quite so enjoyable.

In January of 1929, Babe received some tragic news. His first wife, Helen, had been killed in a fire. Although they hadn't been together for years, he was still saddened by her loss. He asked the press to respect her privacy. In April, he married Claire Hodgson. It was clear to everyone that Babe had settled down.

But even as Babe was happy in his personal life, things were starting to get harder for the Yankees. No ball club can stay on top forever, and in 1929, the Yankees were in transition. Although Ruth and Gehrig still formed a potent combo, New York's pitching staff wasn't as strong. The Yankees were shaken even further by the death of manager Miller Huggins late in the 1929 season. Although Babe and Huggins had clashed, after his 1925 suspension Babe and the manager had grown quite close. It was a huge blow to the team.

Surprisingly, the Philadelphia Athletics were the best team in baseball. Sluggers Jimmie Foxx and Al Simmons were almost as powerful as Gehrig and Ruth, and fireball pitcher Lefty Grove led a terrific pitching staff. The A's took off in 1929 and didn't look back. Philadelphia won three straight pennants and two world championships starting in 1929.

Still, Babe remained one of the most dangerous hitters in baseball. As he grew older, he managed to make small adjustments at the plate to adapt to his slowing reflexes: he used a lighter bat and stood a bit farther away from the plate. In 1929, he became the first man in the history of baseball to hit five hundred home runs in his career. Two years later, he became the first man to hit six hundred.

But Babe and the Yankees really wanted another championship. The thirty-six-year-old Babe realized that at his age, his career as a player would soon come to an end. As early as 1929, after Huggins's death, Babe hoped to be named manager of the Yankees. But the ball club wasn't confident that he had the self-discipline for the job. Babe held on to his hope of becoming the manager sometime in the future. He knew that helping the Yankees win another world championship would help.

In 1932, the Yankees were invigorated by the performance of some younger players, such as catcher Bill Dickey and pitcher Lefty Gomez. For the first time in three years, the team finally had enough pitching depth to overtake the A's and win the pennant.

Few people expected Babe Ruth, at age thirty-seven, to be the star of the World Series against the Chicago Cubs. Babe had hit only forty-one home runs, far fewer than league leader Jimmie Foxx, who was closing in on Babe's home run record with fifty-eight of his own. Babe's legs were giving him trouble, too, and in September he had been hospitalized with stomach trouble. Before the World Series, there was even some speculation that Babe wouldn't be in the Yankees' starting lineup.

When the series began, however, Babe was in his usual spot in the right field and hitting third in the lineup. Although Lou Gehrig had a wonderful World Series, hitting over .500 as the Yankees swept Chicago, all the headlines, as usual, went to Babe Ruth. He did something even he found hard to believe—if he even did it at all.

Former Yankee Mark Koenig had joined the Cubs in midseason and keyed their pennant run. Yet his teammates had voted him only a half share of the World Series money. His old teammates on the Yankees, particularly Babe Ruth, thought the Cubs were being unfair to Koenig. In the first two games in New York, both teams razzed each other from the bench. Babe kept calling the Cubs "cheapskates," and the Chicago players gave it right back to him.

When Babe and the Yankees went to Chicago for game three, he didn't let up. Wrigley Field, the home of the Cubs, was much smaller than Yankee Stadium. During batting practice Babe hit home run after home run into the stands. He told a reporter, "If I could hit here all the time I'd play for half my salary."

When the game started, the bench jockeying

continued. Even Cubs fans got into the act, and Babe kept up a running conversation with Cubs players and fans. It grew worse after his first at bat against pitcher Charlie Root. Babe clubbed a pitch into the stands to give the Yankees a 3–0 lead.

In the fourth inning, Babe gave the Cubs and their supporters something to howl about. He tried to make a shoestring catch and missed the ball. The hit went for a double and the Cubs were able to tie the game 4–4. Cubs fans threw paper and lemons at Babe. They hooted at him unmercifully.

Babe was embarrassed and a little angry. He stepped to the plate to lead off the fifth inning determined to quiet the crowd.

As he approached the plate, he was booed loudly and the Cubs bench called him all sorts of names. Babe listened and then cupped his hands over his mouth and yelled back at them.

The fans started booing even louder. Then he stepped into the batter's box.

Pitcher Charlie Root buzzed a pitch over the heart of the plate and Babe just watched it pass. Then he turned to the Cubs bench and held up one finger, as if to say, *That's one.*

The howling increased. The Cubs and their fans

wanted to see Babe embarrassed and humiliated by a strikeout.

Root threw two more pitches for balls, and again Babe didn't take the bat from his shoulder. It appeared as if he wasn't going to swing. *What is he doing?* the fans thought. He had to swing at something.

Then Root threw another strike. Babe again watched it pass like he didn't have a care in the world. Then he looked at the Cubs bench and held up *two* fingers, as if to say, *Strike two.*

The crowd was roaring at a fever pitch. The Cubs were on the dugout steps screaming at the Bambino. He stepped out of the box and gestured to them as if he were pushing them away, like he was some kind of colossus they couldn't touch.

He turned to the Cubs catcher and said, "It only takes one to hit it." Root yelled something at Babe and he yelled back, "I'm gonna knock the ball down your throat."

Babe was grinning widely. Like a Cheshire cat, his smile was toothy and wide. It stretched across his whole face. And he wouldn't stop. It was driving the Cubs crazy!

Then the Babe gestured again. To some observers it looked as if the gesture was to the Cubs bench. Others thought he waved at Root. Most people were convinced that Babe had pointed to the center-field bleachers, as if to let the entire world know exactly where the ball was going.

Root wound up and threw. This time Babe took a tremendous swing at the pitch. The bat cut through the air with a snap like a rubber band breaking.

Boom!

The sound of the bat hitting the ball echoed over the sounds of the park and silenced the fans. The ball rocketed directly over Root's head and kept rising, growing smaller and smaller. The Cubs center fielder ran straight back and then ran out of room as the ball sailed over his head and deep into the stands in center field.

Babe just watched the ball the entire way. As he jogged toward first base, he started to laugh. He had a choice comment for each Chicago infielder he passed, plus a few things for the Cubs bench as he trotted past third to home.

The Cubs were silent. Babe had spoken in a way no other player in the game could.

On the very next pitch, Lou Gehrig homered, and the Yankees went on to win the game 7–5 to take command of the series. The next day the Yankees ended the Cubs' World Series run and captured another world championship.

But that wasn't the end of the story. Everyone at the park knew that Babe had held up his fingers before hitting the home run, and everyone knew that he had made some kind of gesture before belting the home run.

One newspaper reporter captured the mood of the moment by writing that Babe had pointed to center field before the pitch, then "punched a screaming liner to a spot where no ball had ever been hit before." The blast became known as the "called shot," and soon everyone was saying Babe had pointed to center field before hitting the home run.

Witnesses were divided about whether he actually did point, but the story seemed like something only Babe Ruth could have done, or would even have dared to do. Babe himself claimed that he had pointed "but not [to] a specific spot. I just wanted to give that thing a ride out of the park."

Although film footage turned up later that seemed to indicate Babe didn't exactly point, that hardly matters. The legend of the "called shot" already had a life of its own. And even if he didn't point, there was no question that he waited for one pitch and then hit that pitch out of the park. The incident put a tremendous exclamation point on his wondrous career.

Babe Ruth had already done things on the baseball field no one thought possible, and in doing so

B. Bennett / contributor / Getty Images

BABE HITS A HOME RUN IN THE SAME 1932 WORLD SERIES GAME WHERE HE HIT THE "CALLED SHOT."

had somehow evolved from a sad, lost little boy into one of the most beloved figures in sporting history. Even if Babe didn't point as people claimed he did, there was no question in anyone's mind that if anyone in the history of the game could hit a home run at will, it was Babe Ruth. He was larger than life. He was a living legend.

CHAPTER NINE
1933–1948

HEADING HOME

Not even Babe Ruth could play forever, though. Over the next two seasons, it became clear that his strength and stamina were waning and that his career was winding down. His power was sporadic and his speed had all but left him. The Yankees finished second each season and Babe's performance slowly declined. After hitting .301 with thirty-four home runs in 1933, in 1934 he hit .288 with only twenty-two home runs.

Babe was still the most popular player in baseball. If anything, he was more popular than ever, as fans who had grown up with him now took their children to see him.

On occasion, he could still be the most dynamic player in the game. In the inaugural All-Star Game, played in Chicago in 1933, Babe—who else?—hit the first home run in All-Star Game history.

He still commanded a big salary, but it was now

more than the Yankees felt he was worth. They wanted him to return in 1935, but only as a pinch hitter and at a reduced salary. Babe knew his career as a player was coming to an end, but he hoped that his time with the Yankees wasn't over. He hadn't given up his dream of becoming the team's manager.

There was just one problem. The Yankees were happy with current manager Joe McCarthy. When Babe asked if they were thinking about replacing McCarthy and if he had a chance for the job, he was told no. Although Babe's behavior had improved dramatically, the owners worried that he wouldn't be able to command respect from his players. After all, everyone knew that for most of his career he had broken the rules.

"That's all I need to know," said Babe when told of the club's decision.

Sadly, no other team seemed interested in hiring Babe as manager, either. While his future hung in the balance, he traveled to Japan to help popularize baseball in that country. The game had caught on in Japan and Babe was greeted like a conquering hero, but when he returned to America in February, he still didn't know if or where he would be playing in 1935.

Then Judge Emil Fuchs, owner of the Boston Braves, approached Jacob Ruppert and asked if he would sell the Babe's contract. The Braves were desperate to draw fans. Fuchs offered the great Bambino the chance to play one more season, as well as a position as a team vice president and assistant manager. He even said he would consider making Babe manager in the near future.

"If he can better himself elsewhere," Ruppert responded to Fuchs's offer, "the Yankees won't stand in his way." Ruppert agreed to release Babe. If Babe wanted to sign with the Braves he was now free to do so.

Babe met with Fuchs and accepted the Braves' offer. He opened the season in the Braves outfield before 25,000 freezing fans in Boston. Babe, now forty years old, was magnificent. He hit a two-run homer and made a diving catch as the Braves won 4–1. Boston fans went crazy. Even at the end of his career, he could still amaze the crowd.

Then he stopped hitting. Over the next month, he got only two more hits and was bothered by a cold. He also found out that his title as team vice president was just for show, and that Braves manager Bill McKechnie had little use for an "assistant manager."

In early May, a frustrated Babe wanted to retire. But Fuchs talked him into staying with the team through its next road trip. Thousands of fans had already bought tickets to see him play.

Babe reluctantly agreed. Except for one last day in Pittsburgh, he played terribly, but on that day he was as good as he had ever been.

In his first at bat he cracked a two-run home run. In his next trip to the plate he hit another home run. After singling in his third time up, Babe came to bat one last time.

The pitcher was Guy Bush, who had once pitched for the 1932 Cubs. The bases were empty.

Babe Ruth was forty years old. For a ballplayer, he was old and very heavy. He had already decided he would retire in a few days.

But he still had one great swing left in him. Bush threw a junker and Babe hit the pitch on the sweet part of the bat. The ball rocketed into the sky until it was just a small speck. Then it dropped down and down, all the way over the double-decked grandstand in right field at Pittsburgh's Forbes Field. It hit the roof of a house across the street, bounced off another rooftop, and rolled to a stop in a nearby lot. Witnesses later said a young boy walking by saw the rolling ball, picked it up, and went on his way, probably wondering where in the world the baseball had come from. The vacant lot was more than six hundred feet from home plate!

Guy Bush later said, "I've never seen a ball hit so hard before or since." No one had ever even hit a ball onto the roof of the grandstand, much less over it. The blast was the 714th of Babe Ruth's career. It was also his last. It was fitting that the last home run Babe Ruth hit traveled six hundred feet and wowed the crowd.

After the game, Duffy Lewis, a former Red Sox teammate who worked for the Braves, told Babe he should quit at the top and never play another game. But Babe had promised Fuchs he'd finish the road trip. A few days later, in Philadelphia, he struck out in the first inning, then wrenched his knee and had to leave the game. He never played in the major leagues again.

Less than a week later, he told reporters simply, "I'm quitting." He felt the Braves had broken their promises to him. "I'd still like to manage," he added.

But baseball never really found a place for Babe Ruth after retirement. Yet it never forgot him, either. In 1936, the National Baseball Hall of Fame opened in Cooperstown, New York. Only five players—Babe Ruth, Ty Cobb, Walter Johnson, Christy Mathewson, and Honus Wagner—were selected for induction that first season, chosen above everyone else who had ever played the game.

A few years later, in 1939, Babe Ruth coached one season for Brooklyn, but when it became clear they didn't intend to make him manager, he quit again. He spent most of his time with his wife, Claire, playing golf, giving speeches at clinics, and just relaxing.

He returned to Yankee Stadium on July 4, 1939, for Lou Gehrig Appreciation Day. His former teammate was dying of a degenerative disease called amyotrophic lateral sclerosis, or ALS, now commonly known as Lou Gehrig's disease. On July 4, the Yankees honored Gehrig with a day of his own. Babe Ruth gave Lou Gehrig a big hug after Gehrig gave a speech in which he referred to himself as "the luckiest man on the face of the earth" for having the opportunity to play baseball. A few years later, Babe even played himself in a movie based on Gehrig's life.

During World War II, Babe helped raise hundreds of thousands of dollars for the Red Cross and made many appearances in exhibitions, hitting home runs and making people smile like he always had.

In April 1947, baseball commissioner Happy Chandler declared that it was "Babe Ruth Day" all across the country, and Babe was invited to appear at Yankee Stadium again. He'd been sick and was starting to lose weight.

He didn't know it yet, but he was dying.

All his former teammates turned out and so did Johnny Sylvester, the sick young boy Babe had hit a home run for who was now recovered and a grown man. The 58,000 people in Yankee Stadium did their best to show the man who had captured their hearts, the man who had captivated the nation, the greatest player to ever play the game exactly how much he meant to them. Before the game, he spoke to the crowd with a raspy voice:

"The only real game, I think, is baseball," he said. "You have to start from way down at the bottom.... You've got to let it grow up with you, and if you're successful and try hard enough, you're bound to come out on top." He was speaking about the game of baseball, but he could have been describing his own life.

Babe made one more appearance at Yankee Stadium, one year later on the twenty-fifth anniversary of "the House that Ruth Built." He was too ill to speak to the crowd but had one last chance to see his old friends and teammates. Two months later, on August 16, 1948, Babe Ruth died.

But a figure as legendary as Babe Ruth can never truly die. When he retired from baseball he held

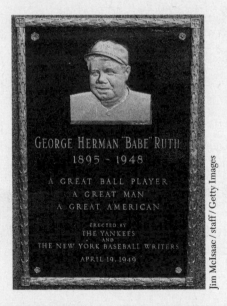

Jim McIsaac / staff / Getty Images

A PLAQUE HONORING BABE COULD BE SEEN AT MONUMENT PARK AT THE OLD YANKEE STADIUM.

virtually every slugging record—most total bases, highest slugging percentage, most extra-base hits, and, of course, the most home runs with a career total of 714. He even led in career strikeouts and walks.

Although some of those records no longer stand, no player since has ever been loved as much as the Babe. Babe Ruth, the tough kid from Baltimore who grew up to become the greatest player in the game, lives on in the heart of every baseball fan. He will never be forgotten.

TURN THE PAGE
FOR MORE
FUN FACTS!

BABE RUTH

GEORGE HERMAN RUTH
(BABE, THE BAMBINO, OR THE SULTAN OF SWAT)

POSITIONS: Outfielder and pitcher

BATS: Left

THROWS: Left

HEIGHT: 6' 2"

WEIGHT: 215 lbs.

BORN: February 6, 1895, in Baltimore, MD

EDUCATION: St. Mary's Industrial School for Boys (Baltimore, MD)

DEBUT: July 11, 1914 (Age 19, 4,196th in MLB history), versus the Cleveland Indians

TEAMS: Red Sox/Yankees/Braves (1914–1935)

LAST GAME: May 30, 1935 (Age 40), versus the Philadelphia Phillies

Inducted into the Hall of Fame by the Baseball Writer's Association of America in 1936. Induction ceremony in Cooperstown was held in 1939.

DIED: August 16, 1948, in New York, NY (Age 53)

BURIED: Gate of Heaven Cemetery, Hawthorne, NY

BABE'S MANY RECORDS

 CAREER HOME RUNS (total of 714)—52 years
SINGLE-SEASON HRs (60 home runs)—41 years

 CONSECUTIVE SCORELESS INNINGS PITCHED IN A WORLD SERIES (29 $^2/_3$)—43 years

 CAREER RBIs (final total of 2214)—41 years
CAREER SLUGGING % (.6897)—Ongoing
CAREER OPS (On-Base plus Slugging)
(1.164)—Ongoing
SINGLE-SEASON RBIs (168)—6 years
SINGLE-SEASON SLUGGING % (.847)—80 years
SINGLE-SEASON OPS (1.379)—82 years

 **CAREER ON-BASE %**
(.474)—22 years
SINGLE-SEASON TOTAL BASES (457)—Ongoing

CAREER BASE ON BALLS (total of 2062)— 81 years

SINGLE-SEASON BASE ON BALLS (total of 150 and 170)—81 years

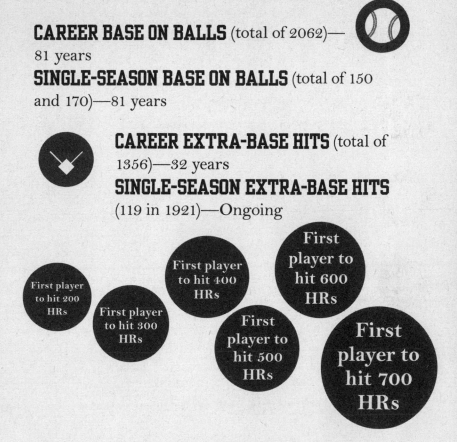

CAREER EXTRA-BASE HITS (total of 1356)—32 years

SINGLE-SEASON EXTRA-BASE HITS (119 in 1921)—Ongoing

First player to hit 200 HRs

First player to hit 300 HRs

First player to hit 400 HRs

First player to hit 500 HRs

First player to hit 600 HRs

First player to hit 700 HRs

HIGHEST BATTING AVERAGE FOR A WORLD SERIES (.625 during 1928)—73 years

CAREER FOR HITS PER 9 INNINGS (6.692 in 1918; 7.113 in 1922–1929)—9 years

MOST HOME RUNS IN A SEASON RECORD HOLDERS

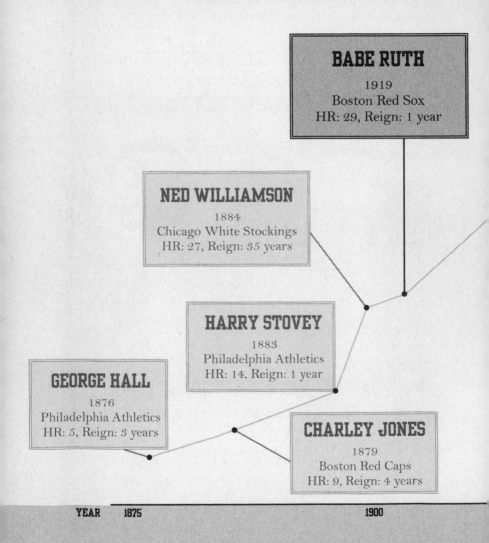

BABE RUTH
1919
Boston Red Sox
HR: 29, Reign: 1 year

NED WILLIAMSON
1884
Chicago White Stockings
HR: 27, Reign: 35 years

HARRY STOVEY
1883
Philadelphia Athletics
HR: 14, Reign: 1 year

GEORGE HALL
1876
Philadelphia Athletics
HR: 5, Reign: 3 years

CHARLEY JONES
1879
Boston Red Caps
HR: 9, Reign: 4 years

YEAR   1875   1900

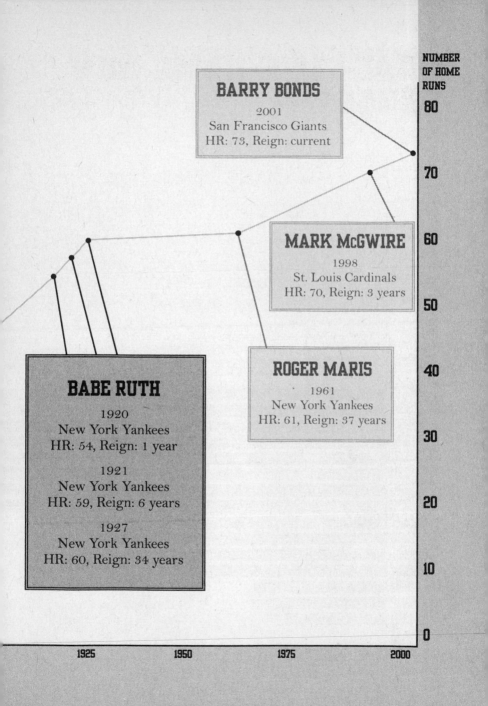

NUMBER
OF HOME
RUNS

BARRY BONDS

2001
San Francisco Giants
HR: 73, Reign: current

MARK McGWIRE

1998
St. Louis Cardinals
HR: 70, Reign: 3 years

BABE RUTH

1920
New York Yankees
HR: 54, Reign: 1 year

1921
New York Yankees
HR: 59, Reign: 6 years

1927
New York Yankees
HR: 60, Reign: 34 years

ROGER MARIS

1961
New York Yankees
HR: 61, Reign: 37 years

80

70

60

50

40

30

20

10

0

1925   1950   1975   2000

ALL-TIME HOME RUN LEADERS

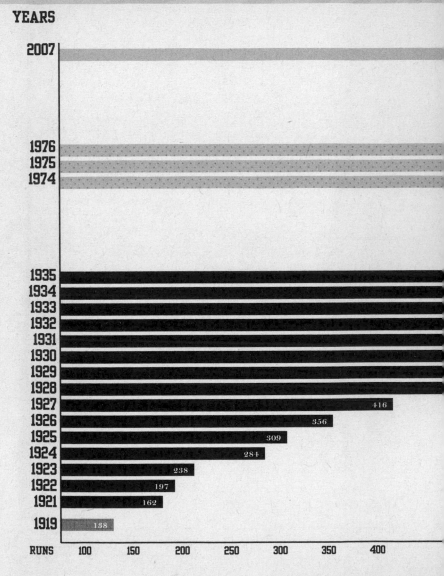

YEARS

2007	
1976	
1975	
1974	
1935	
1934	
1933	
1932	
1931	
1930	
1929	
1928	
1927	416
1926	356
1925	309
1924	284
1923	238
1922	197
1921	162
1919	138

RUNS 100 150 200 250 300 350 400

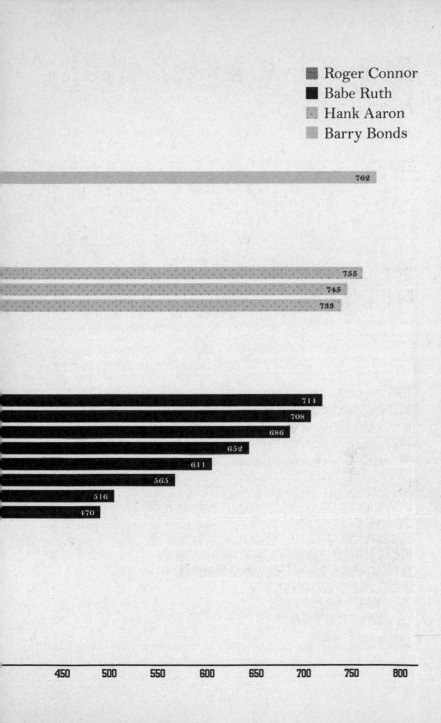

BABE'S TEAMS

BALTIMORE

Age 19

Approx. **20** games

PROVIDENCE

Age 19

Approx. **23** games

BOSTON

Age 19–26

391 games played for the Red Sox

NEW YORK

Age 25–39

2,084 games played for the Yankees

(**404** at the Polo Grounds in Manhattan and

1,680 at Yankee Stadium in the Bronx)

BOSTON BRAVES

Age 40

28 games played for the Braves at what is now
Nickerson Field

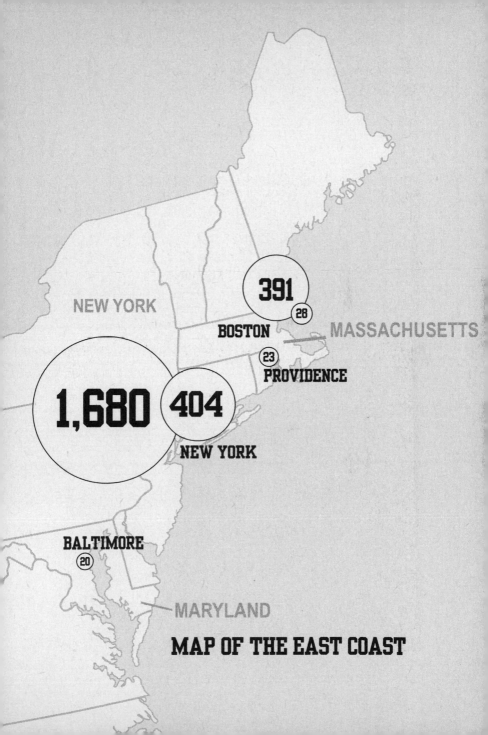

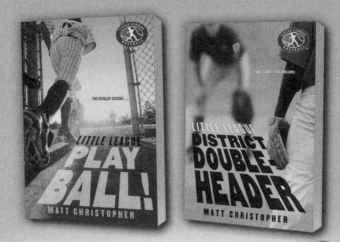

to

ies

For Every
Individual...

The
INDIANAPOLIS PUBLIC
Library

**Renew by Phone
269-5222**

Renew on the Web
www.indypl.org

For General Library Information
please call 275-4100